GREAT AIRCRAFT OF WORLD WAR II

MESSERSCHMITT 109

GREAT AIRCRAFT OF WORLD WAR II
MESSERSCHMITT 109
AN ILLUSTRATED GUIDE SHOWN IN OVER 75 IMAGES

ALFRED PRICE

LORENZ BOOKS

This edition is published by Lorenz Books,
an imprint of Anness Publishing Ltd,
108 Great Russell Street,
London WC1B 3NA;
info@anness.com

www.lorenzbooks.com; www.annesspublishing.com

Anness Publishing has a new picture agency outlet for images for publishing, promotions
or advertising. Please visit our website www.practicalpictures.com for more information.

A CIP catalogue record for this book is available from the British Library.

Publisher: Joanna Lorenz
Senior Editor: Felicity Forster
Production Controller: Rosanna Anness

PUBLISHER'S NOTE
Although the advice and information in this book are believed to be accurate
and true at the time of going to press, neither the authors nor the publisher can
accept any legal responsibility or liability for any errors or omissions that may have
been made nor for any inaccuracies nor for any loss, harm or injury that
comes about from following instructions or advice in this book.

Page 1: **An Me 109 'Caesar' of Fighter Gruppe 152.**
Page 2: **Two 'Emils' of Fighter Geschwader 27 on patrol over the North African desert.**
Page 3: **'Gustav-6' carrying the white fuselage band and wing tips of a unit operating on the Mediterranean front.**
Below: **Me 109 'Gustav-2s' belonging to a tactical reconnaissance Gruppe.**

CONTENTS

INTRODUCTION

Canterbury, Kent, 13.05 hours, 18 August 1940

Above: **Me 109Es of Gerhard Schoepfel's unit, IIIrd Gruppe of Fighter Geschwader 26, pictured in their camouflaged dispersal points at Caffiers near Calais during the Battle of Britain.**

Oberleutnant Gerhard Schoepfel was flying his favourite type of mission. He had eight aerial victories to his credit already, and was leading a free hunting patrol 4 miles (6.5km) high over southern England. It was the sort of mission that did not come his way often enough. With some 25 Me 109Es of IIIrd Gruppe of Fighter Geschwader 26 arrayed in battle formation behind and above him, he felt invincible. His task was to clear a path in front of raiding formations making for the important Fighter Command airfields at Kenley and Biggin Hill. The nearest bombers were some 20 miles (32km) behind him, and they were not his concern. Today, others had the frustrating task of flying close escort for the slow-flying Dorniers and Heinkels to ward off attacks by the Spitfires and Hurricanes. Schoepfel's role was that of a hunter, pure and simple. His orders were to engage and destroy any British fighters he found, and he had complete tactical freedom to do so in any way he chose. Over enemy territory, the German pilot's practised eyes quartered the sky continually and systematically, seeking out his quarry.

■ COVER THE LEADER ■

"Suddenly I noticed a Staffel of Hurricanes underneath me. They were using the English tactics of the period, flying in close formation of threes, climbing in a wide

Above: Oberleutnant Gerhard Schoepfel. At the end of the war, he was credited with 40 aerial victories. (Schoepfel)

spiral. About 1,000m above them I turned with them and managed to get behind the two covering Hurricanes, which were weaving continually."

In deciding his tactics, Schoepfel knew it was important to retain the element of surprise for as long as possible. Several aircraft diving to attack would almost certainly be spotted. But a single aircraft might sneak unobserved into a firing position behind the enemy fighters. The German ace ordered his pilots to remain at high altitude and cover him, while he delivered a lone attack on the formation from out of the sun. The Hurricanes, belonging to No. 501 Squadron were climbing into position to engage the bomber formations nearing the coast. Picking up speed rapidly in the dive, Schoepfel remained unseen as he swung behind one of the two 'weaver' Hurricanes covering the rear of the formation. He placed his sighting graticule over the fighter, loosed off an accurate burst and saw it go down in flames. Then he pulled to one side and repeated the process with the second 'weaver'. Still the formation

Right: The tail of Gerhard Schoepfel's aircraft photographed on the afternoon of 18 August 1940, including the victory bars for the four Hurricanes of No. 501 Squadron.

continued on its ponderous way. The German pilot moved in behind the main formation, fired again and a third Hurricane fell out of the sky.

"The Englishmen continued on their way having noticed nothing. So I pulled behind a fourth machine and took care of him also. But this time I went in too close. When I pressed the firing button, the Englishman was such a short distance in front of my nose that pieces of wreckage struck my propeller. Oil streaming back from the fourth plane spattered over my windscreen and the right side of the cabin, so that I could see nothing. I had to break off the action."

Finally aware of their peril, the surviving Hurricanes broke formation and turned to engage the Messerschmitts diving to support their leader. There followed an inconclusive dogfight without loss to either side. Within a space of four minutes Gerhard Schoepfel, single-handed, had destroyed a third of a squadron of Hurricanes. One pilot was killed, and the other three jumped from their stricken aircraft and landed safely by parachute. In the summer of 1940, both the Luftwaffe and the Me 109 were at the peak of their effectiveness relative to the air forces and fighter types opposing them. Only the Spitfire was as fast as the German fighter, while all the other fighters it encountered in action were a good deal slower. It was a clear indication of Schoepfel's unbounded confidence in his aircraft and his ability that, alone and without hesitation, he took on an entire enemy squadron and emerged victorious from the encounter. Small wonder the very name of Messerschmitt was one that struck fear in Germany's enemies throughout the whole of the Second World War.

MESSERSCHMITT Me 109G-14

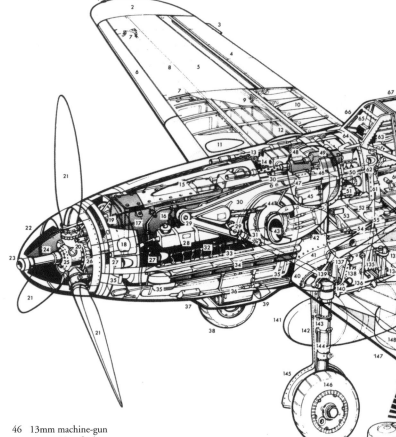

1   Starboard navigation light
2   Starboard wingtip
3   Fixed trim tab
4   Starboard Frise-type aileron
5   Flush-riveted stressed wing-skinning
6   Handley Page leading-edge automatic slot
7   Slot control linkage
8   Slot equalizer rod
9   Aileron control linkage
10 Fabric-covered flap section
11 Wheel fairing
12 Port fuselage machine-gun ammunition-feed fairing
13 Port Rheinmetall-Borsig 13mm MG 131 machine-gun
14 Engine accessories
15 Starboard machine-gun trough
16 Daimler-Benz DB 605AM 12-cylinder inverted-vee liquid-cooled engine
17 Detachable cowling panel
18 Oil filter access
19 Oil tank
20 Propeller pitch-change mechanism
21 VDM electrically operated constant-speed propeller
22 Spinner
23 Engine-mounted cannon muzzle
24 Blast tube
25 Propeller hub
26 Spinner back plate
27 Auxiliary cooling intakes
28 Cooling header tank
29 Anti-vibration rubber engine mounting pads
30 Elektron forged engine bearer
31 Engine bearer support strut attachment
32 Plug leads
33 Exhaust manifold fairing strip
34 Ejector exhausts
35 Cowling fasteners
36 Oil cooler
37 Oil cooler intake
38 Starboard mainwheel
39 Oil cooler outlet flap
40 Wing root fillet
41 Wing/fuselage fairing
42 Firewall/bulkhead
43 Supercharger air intake
44 Supercharger assembly
45 20mm cannon magazine drum

46 13mm machine-gun ammunition feed
47 Engine bearer upper attachment
48 Ammunition feed fairing
49 13mm Rheinmetall-Borsig MG 131 machine-gun breeches
50 Instrument panel
51 20mm Mauser MG 151/20 cannon breech
52 Heelrests
53 Rudder pedals
54 Undercarriage emergency retraction cables
55 Fuselage frame
56 Wing/fuselage fairing
57 Undercarriage emergency retraction headwheel (outboard)
58 Tail trim handwheel (inboard)

59 Seat harness
60 Throttle lever
61 Control column
62 Cockpit ventilation inlet
63 Revi 16B reflector gunsight (folding)
64 Armoured windshield frame
65 Anti-glare gunsight screen
66 90mm armourglass windscreen
67 Galland-type clear-vision hinged canopy

68 Framed armourglass head/back panel
69 Canopy contoured frame
70 Canopy hinges (starboard)
71 Canopy release catch
72 Pilot's bucket-type seat (8mm back armour)
73 Underfloor contoured fuel tank (88 imp gal/400 litres of 87 octane B4)
74 Fuselage frame
75 Circular access panel

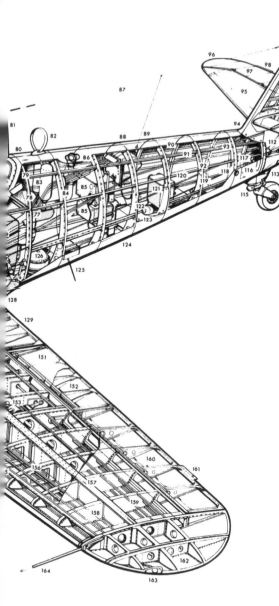

134 Spar/fuselage lower pin joint (vertical)
135 Flaps equalizer rod
136 Rüstsatz R3 auxiliary fuel tank ventral rack
137 Undercarriage electrical interlock
138 Wing horizontal pin forward pick-up
139 Undercarriage retraction jack mechanism
140 Undercarriage pivot-bevel
141 Auxiliary fuel tank (Rüstsatz R3) of 66 imp gal (3,000 litre) capacity
142 Mainwheel leg fairing
143 Mainwheel oleo leg
144 Brake lines
145 Mainwheel fairing
146 Port mainwheel
147 Leading-edge skin
148 Port mainwheel well
149 Wing spar
150 Flap actuating linkage
151 Fabric-covered control surfaces
152 Slotted flap structure
153 Leading-edge slot actuating mechanism
154 Slot equalizer rod
155 Handley Page automatic leading-edge slot
156 Wing stringers
157 Spar flange decrease
158 Wing ribs
159 Flush-riveted stressed wing- skinning
160 Metal-framed Frise-type aileron
161 Fixed trim tab
162 Wingtip construction
163 Port navigation light
164 Angled pitot head
165 Rüstsatz R6 optional underwing cannon gondola
166 14-point plug connection
167 Electrical junction box
168 Cannon rear mounting bracket
169 20mm Mauser MG 151 20mm cannon
170 Cannon front mounting bracket
171 Ammunition feed chute
172 Ammunition magazine drum
173 Underwing panel
174 Gondola fairing
175 Cannon barrel

93 Tail trimming cables
94 Tailfin root fairing
95 Starboard fixed tailplane
96 Elevator balance
97 Starboard elevator
98 Geared elevator tab
99 All-wooden tailfin construction
100 Aerial attachment
101 Rudder upper hinge bracket
102 Rudder post
103 Fabric-covered wooden rudder structure
104 Geared rudder tab
105 Rear navigation light
106 Port elevator
107 Geared elevator tab
108 Tailplane structure
109 Rudder actuating linkage
110 Elevator control horn
111 Elevator connecting rod
112 Elevator control quadrant
113 Tailwheel leg cuff
114 Castoring non-retractable tailwheel
115 Lengthened tailwheel/leg
116 Access panel
117 Tailwheel shock-strut
118 Lifting point
119 Rudder cable
120 Elevator cables
121 First-aid pack
122 Air bottles
123 Fuselage access panel
124 Bottom keel (connector stringer)
125 Ventral IFF aerial
126 Master compass
127 Elevator control linkage
128 Wing root fillet
129 Camber-changing flap
130 Ducted coolant radiator
131 Wing stringers
132 Wing rear pick-up point
133 Spar/fuselage upper pin joint (horizontal)

76 Tail trimming cable conduit
77 Wireless leads
78 MW50 (methanel/water) tank (25 imp gal/114 litres capacity)
79 Handhold
80 Fuselage decking
81 Aerial mast
82 D/F loop
83 Oxygen cylinders (three)
84 Filler pipe
85 Wireless equipment packs (FuG 16ZY communications and FuG 25a IFF)
86 Main fuel filler cap
87 Aerial
88 Fuselage top keel (connector stringer)
89 Aerial lead-in
90 Fuselage skin plating sections
91 U-stringers
92 Fuselage frames (monocoque construction)

The story of the Messerschmitt 109 began in 1934, more than a year before the German government revealed the existence of the clandestine air force that it had built up. Early that year, the Air Ministry issued a requirement for an advanced monoplane fighter to replace the Heinkel 51 and Arado 68 biplanes then about to enter service, and invited aircraft companies to submit designs.

The early 1930s saw rapid advances in aviation technology, which revealed themselves most clearly in the design of fighter planes. The new generation of fighters was quite different in shape and performance from those that had gone before. Out went the fabric-covered strut-braced biplane with its open cockpit and fixed undercarriage. In its place came the sleek low-wing monoplane with an all-metal structure, enclosed cockpit and a retractable undercarriage. These new fighters were much faster than their predecessors in the climb, in the dive and in level flight. Also, in their developed versions, they were more heavily armed.

Chief designer Willi Messerschmitt had no previous experience of designing fighter aircraft

At that time, the Bavarian Aircraft Company (Bayerische Flugzeugwerke) at Augsburg was a little-known aircraft firm with about 500 employees. It had never built a military aircraft of its own design, though it was turning out small batches of planes built under licence for the Luftwaffe. Willi Messerschmitt, the company's brilliant young chief designer, had no previous experience of designing a fighter. He did have great flair and originality, however, and he was very ambitious. When he saw the Luftwaffe requirement he jumped at the chance to turn his hand to a state-of-the-art fighter plane.

Messerschmitt's new fighter employed almost every innovation of the period. It was a clean-lined all-metal low-wing monoplane with a retractable undercarriage and an enclosed cockpit. To keep the landing speed to reasonable limits, the small wing was fitted with retractable flaps and leading-edge slots. Messerschmitt designed the fighter around the new 610hp Junkers Jumo 210 engine. Work on the airframe advanced more rapidly than that on the power plant, however, and it was clear that the latter would not be ready in time. Messerschmitt had to look elsewhere for an engine to get his prototype into the air. Ironically, in view of later events, his choice of engine was a 695hp Rolls-Royce Kestrel imported from Great Britain.

Opposite: Ground crewmen pictured reloading the wing and engine-mounted 7.9mm machine-guns of a 'Caesar' of IIIrd Gruppe of Fighter Geschwader 51. Scrupulous cleanliness was necessary for this operation, since any grit or dirt on the rounds was liable to cause a stoppage during firing. *Below:* The first prototype Me 109 ground-running its Rolls-Royce Kestrel engine, at about the time of its maiden flight in September 1935. (via Ethell)

MESSERSCHMITT 109 B-1

Type Single-seat interceptor fighter

Armament Two Rheinmetall-Borsig 7.9mm machine-guns mounted on top of the engine and synchronized to fire through the airscrew (500 rounds per gun)

Power plant One Junkers Jumo 210 Da inverted V-12 liquid-cooled engine developing 635hp for take-off

Dimensions Span 32ft 4½in (9.87m); length 28ft (8.55m)

Weight Normal operational take-off 4,741lb (2,150kg)

Performance Maximum speed 289mph at 13,100ft (465km/hr at 4,000m); service ceiling 26,900ft (8,200m)

MESSERSCHMITT 109 C-1

Type Single-seat interceptor fighter

Armament Four Rheinmetall-Borsig MG 17 7.9mm machine-guns; two synchronized to fire through the airscrew (500 rounds per gun), two mounted in wings (420rpg)

Power plant Junkers Jumo 210 Ga inverted V-12 liquid-cooled engine developing 700hp for take-off; this and subsequent versions were fitted with direct fuel injection engines

Dimensions Span 32ft 4in (9.87m); length 28ft (8.55m)

Weight Normal operational take-off 5,060lb (2,295kg)

Performance Maximum speed 292mph (470km/hr) at 14,770ft (4,500m); service ceiling 27,570ft (8,400m)

Initially called the Bayerische Flugzeugwerke (Bf) 109, the new fighter made its maiden flight in September 1935. That was one month before the prototype Hurricane, and six months before the prototype Spitfire – its two main rivals during the early part of the forthcoming conflict.

The Arado, Heinkel and Focke Wulf companies also built prototypes of monoplane fighters for the Luftwaffe design competition. Messerschmitt's more ambitious design quickly demonstrated that it had a clear edge over the other three, however. Its maximum speed of 290mph (467km/hr) was 17mph (27km/hr) faster than that of its nearest rival, and its handling characteristics were also superior.

Below: Line-up of early-production Me 109 'Bertas' awaiting delivery at the Bayerische Flugzeugwerke factory at Augsburg early in 1937. At this time, this aircraft was the most potent fighter in service anywhere in the world. (via Schliephake)

Above: An Me 109 'Caesar' of Fighter
Gruppe 152.

■ INTO PRODUCTION ■

Following the service trials, the
Luftwaffe placed an order for ten more
Me 109 prototypes. A second prototype, powered by the Jumo 21 OA
engine, joined the test programme in
January 1936. In the autumn of 1936,
the Luftwaffe announced that the Me
109 was to be its standard single-
engined fighter type. The Me 109B, the
'Berta', was the initial production
variant. It was powered by the Jumo
210 engine and carried an armament of
three (later four) 7.9mm machine-guns.

In February 1937, production Me
109Bs began emerging from the
Augsburg factory. The first Luftwaffe
unit to receive the new fighter was IInd

Gruppe of Fighter Geschwader 132
based at Jueterbog near Berlin.

Early in 1938, the next major version
of the Me 109 appeared, the Me 109C
'Caesar'. This featured several detailed
improvements, and its Jumo 210 engine

was fitted with fuel injection. The initial
version carried four machine-guns, two
on top of the engine and one in each
wing close to the root. The 'Caesar' was
built in moderately large numbers, and
the variant equipped several fighter units.

MESSERSCHMITT 109 D-1

Type Single-seat interceptor fighter
Armament Two Rheinmetall-Borsig MG 17 7.9mm machine-guns mounted on top of the
engine synchronized to fire through the airscrew (500 rounds per gun); one Oerlikon MG
FF 20mm cannon mounted under the engine and firing through the spinner (60 rounds)
Power plant One Daimler-Benz DB 600Aa inverted V-12 liquid-cooled engine
developing 986hp for take-off
Dimensions Span 32ft 4in (9.87m); length 28ft 2in (8.60m)
Weight Normal operational take-off 5,336lb (2,420kg)
Performance Maximum speed 356mph (574km/hr) at 11,490ft (3,500m);
service ceiling 32,800ft (10,000m)

Following hard on the heels of the
'Caesar' came the Me 109D 'Dora'. This
was fitted with the new Daimler-Benz
600 engine which developed 960 horse
power. The more powerful engine gave

The fine performance of the 'Dora' was undermined by difficulties with the DB 600 engine

greatly enhanced performance, and the
'Dora' could achieve a maximum speed
of 356mph at 11,400ft (574km/hr at
3,500m). This variant also had greater
fire power than its predecessors, with a
20mm cannon firing through the propeller spinner and two machine-guns
mounted on top of the engine cowling.
The DB 600 engine suffered serious
teething troubles, however, and despite
its fine performance, the 'Dora' was not

MESSERSCHMITT 109 E-1

Type Single-seat general-purpose fighter
Armament Four Rheinmetall-Borsig MG 17 7.9mm machine-guns in fuselage and wings;
or two MG17 machine-guns and two MG FF cannon; some aircraft were modified to carry
a rack for a single 110lb (45kg) bomb
Power plant One Daimler-Benz DB 601A inverted V-12 liquid-cooled engine
developing 1,175hp for take-off
Dimensions Span 32ft 4in (9.87m); length 28ft 4in (8.64m)
Weight Normal operational take-off 5,535lb (2,510kg)
Performance Maximum speed 356mph at 13,130ft (573km/hr at 4,000m);
service ceiling 34,450ft (10,500m)

Above: The Heinkel 51 biplane was the main fighter type serving with the Condor Legion during the early stages of the Civil War in Spain. It was outclassed by the Soviet-built fighter types that it came up against.

popular with pilots. Fewer than 200 were built before this variant passed out of production.

In September 1938, the so-called Munich Crisis broke, as a result of Adolf Hitler's claim that the Sudetenland area of Czechoslovakia should be incorporated into Germany. For a time, it seemed that Great Britain might go to war to help the Czechs retain this territory, but in the end the British prime minister Neville Chamberlain acceded to Hitler's demand. Several commentators have said that the move was necessary to allow Britain time to re-arm. They neglect the fact that the Luftwaffe, too, was in no state to engage in a major conflict. Its fighter force possessed 583 Me 109s of all versions, of which 510 were serviceable. Most of these aircraft were the 'Bertas', with smaller numbers

of the later 'Caesar' and 'Dora' variants. Eight fighter Gruppen had equipped or were in the process of re-equipping with the Me 109. The rest operated outdated biplane fighter types. The Luftwaffe bomber force was no better placed to fight a major war. At the time, many people were frightened by the barrage of misleading German propaganda regarding the size and invincibility of the Luftwaffe. Even now, in the present-day 21st century, these canards are still repeated.

The next version of the Me 109, the first built in really large numbers, was the 'Emil' powered by the new Daimler-Benz 601 engine. Based on the DB 600 engine that powered the 'Dora', the new engine was fitted with fuel injection and a more effective supercharger. Most important of all, it was far more reliable than the earlier engine. The initial batches of Me 109Es reached the Luftwaffe early in 1939. The main production version was armed with two 7.9mm machine-guns in the fuselage and two 20mm cannon in the wings.

■ MESSERSCHMITT AG ■

With the success of the new fighter assured, the management of the Bayerische Flugzeugwerke decided to capitalize on the international reputation won by its now-famous chief designer, and so they appointed Willi Messerschmitt to the posts of Chairman and Managing Director, and changed the company's name to Messerschmitt AG. The firm's two factories were turning out the fighter in large numbers, yet there were insufficient numbers to meet the needs of the expanding Luftwaffe. Four other aircraft companies, Arado, Erla, Fieseler and Focke Wulf, were producing the Me 109E under licence. Production of the fighter reached 130 per month, and it quickly replaced most of the earlier versions in front-line units.

■ IN ACTION IN SPAIN ■

In the summer of 1936, civil war broke out in Spain. General Franco, the Nationalist leader, appealed to Adolf Hitler for help in his revolt against the left-wing government. This was soon forthcoming, and the Luftwaffe dispatched a force, the Condor Legion, to fight alongside the Nationalists. Meanwhile, the Soviet Union had been supplying aircraft to Spain's Republican government. When the Luftwaffe began operations over Spain, its pilots found that the Soviet-built Polikarpov I-16 monoplane had a clear edge in performance over their Heinkel 51 biplanes.

The new 109s of the Condor Legion were operated from a primitive airfield near Seville

---

Generalmajor Hugo Sperrle, the commander of the Condor Legion, impressed on his superiors the need to get Me 109s into the theatre as rapidly as possible. To test the new fighter under combat conditions, late in 1936 the Luftwaffe shipped three Me 109 prototypes to Spain. These operated from a primitive airfied near Seville, and there were severe problems. Each of the handmade prototypes had components unique to itself, which made it difficult to keep

Below: The Soviet Polikarpov I-16 was the best fighter operated by the Nationalist Air Force in Spain. It was clearly superior to the He 51, and came as a shock to the German pilots when they first met it over Spain.

them serviceable. After a few weeks, and without seeing action, the fighters returned to Germany.

■ THE 109 TRIUMPHS ■

The trial highlighted the need for better ground support for the Me 109, if it was to perform effectively in action. Several Luftwaffe pilots flew the prototypes in Spain, and they had no doubt that the Me 109 was superior to any of the Soviet-built fighters opposing them.

As noted in the previous chapter, production Me 109 'Bertas' began to emerge from the Augsburg factory in February 1937. Sixteen of these machines were loaded in crates on a freighter which delivered them to the Condor Legion.

The first unit in Spain to re-equip with the Me 109B was the 2nd Staffel of Fighter Gruppe 88. When it became operational in April 1937 there was a lull in the ground fighting, and initially the new fighter saw little action. Then, in July, the Republican forces launched a powerful offensive near Madrid. The Me 109 Staffel joined the battle, escorting Junkers 52 bombers delivering attacks on Republican troop positions.

As predicted, the Me 109 proved greatly superior to the Soviet-built I-16. It was faster in level flight, had a higher operational ceiling and was much faster in the dive. For its part, the I-16 was more manoeuvrable, especially at altitudes below 10,000ft (3,048m). Republican fighter pilots tried to lure the Messerschmitts into turning fights below 10,000ft, but with little success. German fighter pilots soon learned that their machine's better performance at altitude gave them the advantage of being able to accept or refuse combat, as they chose.

The new German fighter carried radios which might have been very useful during air-to-air actions. The sets gave such poor reception, however, that many pilots flew with them turned off.

The Me 109s would deliver a series of high-speed diving attacks to break up the enemy

---

Normally the Me 109s would patrol at altitudes between 16,000ft (4,877m) and 20,000ft (6,096m), which gave them a substantial height advantage over their opponents. On sighting enemy aircraft, the German formation leader would usually move his force into an attacking position above the prey. The Messerschmitts then delivered a series of high-speed diving attacks, pulling up and zooming back to altitude after each. They repeated the process until the

Above: The arrival of the Me 109B in Spain in the spring of 1937 gave German pilots a machine in which they could engage the I-16 with confidence. This example belonged to 2nd Staffel of Fighter Gruppe 88, and wears the markings carried by aircraft of the Condor Legion.

enemy formation broke up, or the German fighters ran low on fuel or ammunition. Provided the Me 109s maintained their high speed and did not get drawn into turning fights, they were almost unbeatable.

Some of the fiercest aerial fighting over Spain took place early in 1938, during the Republican offensive near Teruél. By then both Staffeln of Fighter Gruppe 88 had re-equipped with the Me 109. On 7 February, Hauptmann Gotthardt Handrick, the Gruppe commander, was leading his unit during a bomber escort mission. Over the battle area he sighted a formation of 22 Soviet-built Tupolev SB-2 bombers moving in to attack a Nationalist troop position. Seeing no Republican fighters in the area, he led a concerted attack on the enemy bombers.

Several of the latter were shot down, and when I-16s finally arrived on the scene, they too suffered losses. The Me 109s destroyed ten enemy bombers and two fighters, without loss to themselves.

Elsewhere that day, another Me 109 pilot fought a noteworthy action.

Leutnant Wilhelm Balthasar shot down three bombers and a fighter within six minutes

Leutnant Wilhelm Balthasar delivered a succession of diving attacks on an escorted bomber formation and short down three bombers and a fighter, all within a space of six minutes.

The Me 109 achieved striking success over Spain, although the number of these fighters sent to fight in the conflict was never large. Up to December 1938, only 55 'Bertas', 'Caesars' and 'Doras' had reached Spain and only 37 were currently on the strength of Fighter Gruppe 88. However, such was the 109's superiority that these few aircraft had been sufficient to establish air supremacy over the dntire country.

In March 1939, after suffering a succession of major reverses, the Republicans were forced to surrender. Following the cessation of hostilities, the Condor Legion returned home to Germany, leaving behind some 50 Me 109s for incorporation in General Franco's Air Force.

■ POISED FOR POLAND ■

By the summer of 1939, Adolf Hitler judged that he had gained as much as he could in Europe by bluff alone. To advance his aims further, he would have to demonstrate Germany's military might and commit its armed forces. Now his forces were poised to launch an all-out onslaught against Poland. In the next chapter, we shall observe how the Me 109 units fared during the early months of the Second World War.

On 1 September 1939, German ground forces invaded Poland, with powerful support from the Luftwaffe. At that time, the Me 109 force comprised 24 Gruppen and five independent Staffeln, with a total of nearly 1,100 fighters. More than two-thirds of the units flew the 'Emil'; the rest operated the older 'Berta', 'Caesar' and 'Dora' versions.

Only about one-fifth of the Me 109 force, five of the 24 Gruppen operating the type, was earmarked to take part in the campaign in Poland. The other units remained at their airfields in western Germany, ready to meet a possible onslaught from the Royal Air Force and the French Air Force. There was no large-scale Allied reaction, however, and the German fighters saw little action. The relatively small proportion of Me 109s assigned to support the attack on Poland proved quite sufficient to counter the meagre forces at the disposal of the Polish Air Force. The latter possessed only about 300 combat planes, almost all of them outdated types. The PZL 11, the most modern Polish fighter type then in service, had a maximum speed of only 242mph (389km/hr). It was no match even for the early versions of the Me 109. After a few days, the Polish Air Force was out of the fight, and unable to give any assistance to its hardpressed army. Two weeks into the campaign, the Luftwaffe felt sufficiently confident to move two Me 109 Gruppen from Poland to bolster the air defences in the west. On 28 September, the Polish forces laid down their arms and the campaign came to an end.

In the west, the aerial activity was on a small scale, as each side probed the other's strengths and weaknesses. On 30 September, the Royal Air Force learned a

Left: Instrument panel of an Me 109 'Emil'. Although the cockpit was cramped and the view of the outside restricted, pilots came to love the machine as a highly capable air superiority fighter.

Me 109 FRONT-LINE UNITS, 2 SEPTEMBER 1939

Unit	Aircraft total	Aircraft serviceable
Tactical Development Division		
Tactical Development (Lehr) Geschwader 2		
Staff Flight	3	3 Me 109E*
I. Gruppe	36	34 Me 109E*
10. Staffel	12	9 Me 109E
Air Fleet 1 (NE Germany)		
Fighter Geschwader 1		
I. Gruppe	54	54 Me 109E*
Fighter Geschwader 2		
II. Gruppe	42	39 Me 109E
10. Staffel	9	9 Me 109C, night-fighting unit
Fighter Geschwader 3		
Staff Flight	3	3 Me 109E
I. Gruppe	48	42 Me 109E
Fighter Geschwader 20		
I. Gruppe	21	20 Me 109E
Fighter Geschwader 21		
I. Gruppe	29	28 Me 109C and E*
Destroyer Geschwader 1		
II. Gruppe	36	36 Me 109B* (a)
Destroyer Geschwader 2		
I. Gruppe	44	40 Me 109D* (a)
Air Fleet 2 (NW Germany)		
Fighter Geschwader 26		
I. Gruppe	48	48 Me 109E
II. Gruppe	48	44 Me 109E
10. Staffel	10	8 Me 109C, night-fighting unit
Destroyer Geschwader 26		
I. Gruppe	52	46 Me 109B and D (a)
II. Gruppe	48	47 Me 109B and D (a)
III. Gruppe	48	44 Me 109B and C (a)
Air Fleet 3 (SW Germany)		
Fighter Geschwader 51		
I. Gruppe	47	39 Me 109E
Fighter Geschwader 52		
I. Gruppe	39	34 Me 109E
Fighter Geschwader 53		
I. Gruppe	51	39 Me 109E
II. Grupp	43	41 Me 109E
Fighter Geschwader 70		
I. Gruppe	24	24 Me 109E
Fighter Geschwader 71		
I. Gruppe	39	18 Me 109C and E
Destroyer Geschwader 52		
I. Gruppe	44	43 Me 109B (a)
Air Fleet 4 (SE Germany)		
Fighter Geschwader 76		
I. Gruppe	49	45 Me 109E
Fighter Geschwader 77		
I. Gruppe	50	43 Me 109E
II. Gruppe	50	36 Me 109E
Destroyer Geschwader 76		
II. Gruppe	40	39 Me 109B and C
Assigned to German Navy		
Traegergruppe 186		
5., 6. Staffeln	24	24 Me 109C (b)

(a) These units had been formed to operate the Me 110 twin-engined fighter, but until these became available they operated Me 109s.
(b) Unit operating standard Me 109Cs, formed to train pilots earmarked to operate the Me 109T from the aircraft carrier *Graf Zeppelin* when she was completed.
* Units marked with an asterisk took part in the campaign in Poland.

IN ACTION OVER FRANCE

"Relatively few Me 109s were lost in combat and only at the end of the campaign, during the Dunkirk evacuation, was there much in the way of fighter-versus-fighter combat. During the campaign in France it was difficult to compare our [Me] 109 with the French Morane or Curtiss fighters, because I never had a dogfight with either of them. I saw only one Morane during the entire campaign and it was disappearing in the distance. Our Geschwader had very little dogfighting experience until the Dunkirk action, where we met the Royal Air Force for the first time in numbers. Our pilots came back with the highest respect for the [new] enemy."

OBERLEUTNANT JULIUS NEUMANN, ME 109 PILOT, FIGHTER GESCHWADER 27

Above: Me 109 'Emil' of Fighter Geschwader 27 pictured early in the war. The oversized markings on the wings were to assist recognition, following a series of incidents when aircraft had been engaged in error by 'friendly' forces.

hard lesson when five Fairey Battle light bombers flew a daylight armed reconnaissance mission over the Saarbrucken area. Me 109s of Fighter Geschwader 53 intercepted the force and shot down four bombers without loss to themselves. Towards the end of the year, the Me 109 again showed its effectiveness as a bomber-destroyer. On 18 December 1939, a force of Vickers Wellingtons flew an armed reconnaissance mission off the coast near Wilhelmshaven, intending to attack any German warships located at sea. The 24 bombers flew in close formation and depended on their combined

Right: A pilot boards his Me 109 'Emil' for a scramble take-off. The aircraft, which bears the 'Scalded Cat' insignia of Fighter Geschwader 20, was pictured during the summer of 1939.

crossfire to deter fighter attacks. Thirty-four Me 109s, drawn from Fighter Geschwader 26 and 77 and Destroyer Geschwader 1, engaged the bombers, together with 16 Me 110s. The German fighters pressed home their attacks despite heavy return fire, and shot down 12 of the Wellingtons. Two more bombers suffered such severe damage that they crashed on landing. For their part, the Wellingtons' gunners shot down only two Me 109s. After this action, the RAF made the policy decision that in future its attacks on targets in

Germany would take place almost exclusively at night.

On 10 May 1940, German forces launched their long-prepared offensive in the west. By that time there were 1,346 Me 109s serving with the front-line units, of which just over 1,000 were serviceable. Three-quarters of these aircraft were assigned to support

Everywhere the Me 109 reigned supreme, with no effective opposition

the offensive, while the rest remained in position to defend targets in Germany. The Luftwaffe quickly established air superiority over the Dutch, Belgian and French Air Forces, and over the Royal Air Force units based in France. Everywhere, the Me 109 reigned supreme, with no effective fighter opposition. Without hindrance from the air or the ground, Luftwaffe bombers and dive-bombers carried out destructive attacks on airfields and other targets ahead of the fast-moving Panzer thrusts.

At the end of May, the German advances pushed the battle front to within range of RAF fighter units flying from bases in southern England. Only during the Dunkirk evacuation was there any serious fighter-versus-fighter combat.

In the course of the evacuation, the Luftwaffe learned the

FIRST PHASE OF THE BATTLE OF BRITAIN

Typical of the scrappy actions of the period was that on 13 July, when a convoy of freighters passed through the Strait of Dover. Half a dozen Junkers 87 'Stuka' dive-bombers were attacking the ships when they were engaged by 11 Hurricanes of No. 56 Squadron.

"Unfortunately for them [the Hurricanes], they slid into position directly between the Stukas and our close-escort Messerschmitts. We opened fire, and at once three Hurricanes separated from the formation, two dropping and one gliding down to the water smoking heavily. At that instant I saw a Stuka diving in an attempt to reach the French coast. It was chased by a single Hurricane. Behind the Hurricane was a 109, and behind that, a second Hurricane, all of the fighters firing at the aircraft in front. I saw the deadly dangerous situation and rushed down. There were five aircraft diving in a line towards the water. The Stuka was badly hit and both crewmen wounded, it crashed on the beach near Wissant. The leading Messerschmitt, flown by Feldwebel John, shot down the first Hurricane into the water, its right wing appearing above the waves like the dorsal fin of a shark before it sank. My Hurricane dropped like a stone close to the one that John had shot down."

Major Josef Foezoe, Leading Me 109s Of Fighter Geschwader 51 Escorting the Stukas

[No. 56 Squadron lost two Hurricanes destroyed and two damaged. On the German side, two Ju 87s were seriously damaged, but Fighter Geschwader 51 suffered no losses.]

same hard lesson as that impressed on the RAF earlier: bombers operating by day without fighter escort could expect heavy losses if they came under attack from well-handled enemy fighters. From then on, the Me 109 force would fly an increasingly large proportion of its missions in the fighter escort role.

■ BATTLE OF BRITAIN ■

The Battle of Britain was the first major action in which Me 109s confronted similar numbers of enemy fighters of comparable performance and flown by pilots with equal determination and skill.

During the Battle of Britain, Me 109 fighter units flew three types of opera-

tion in support of German bombers. First, and most popular with the German pilots, was the free hunting sweep across enemy territory. Its purpose was to break up the defending fighter formations and chase them out of the area, to clear the sky for a bomber formation coming behind. German pilots assigned to this mission had full tactical freedom to engage and pursue RAF fighters as they wished. Second, and slightly less popular, were the 'intermediate escort' operations. In this case, the fighters stayed with their assigned bomber formation until enemy fighters approached their charges, and only then were they free to break away and go into action. Third, and least popular of all, were the close escort operations which occupied the greater part of the fighter force during any large-scale attack. German fighter units assigned to this role had to remain with their allotted bomber formation at all times. Frequently the Me 109s would drive the Spitfires or Hurricanes away from the bombers, but had then to break off the pursuit and return to positions close to their allocated bomber unit. The British fighters would then return to the

Below: A pair of 'Emils' in factory markings, probably photographed during a delivery flight to a Luftwaffe aircraft park.

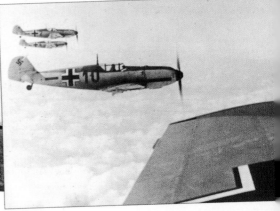

Me 109 VERSUS SPITFIRE AND HURRICANE

"I cannot compare the Me 109 with the Spitfire or the Hurricane – I never flew either of those. We were told that there was no better fighter in the world than the 109 and we believed it. Why shouldn't we – it was certainly a very effective fighter. We knew that the Spitfire and the Hurricane were good fighters too and thought they might be closely comparable with our aircraft. So everything depended on the tactics used and how experienced and aggressive the pilots were. Of course, the RAF had some young and inexperienced pilots. But we had the feeling that there was a strong backbone of very well-trained and experienced pilots. The longer-serving RAF pilots had considerable flying experience. We in the Luftwaffe did not have this advantage. Very few of those who fought on our side in the Battle of Britain had more than four years' flying experience. Overall, we felt that we were dealing with an aircraft-pilot combination as good as our own."

OBERLEUTNANT JULIUS NEUMANN, ME 109 PILOT, FIGHTER GESCHWADER 27

Left: Julius Neumann pictured in the cockpit of the Me 109 at the RAF Museum at Hendon in 1979. He recalled, "Immediately I sat in the cockpit I felt at home. Everything came easily to hand. Had the tank been full and there been enough room in front of me, I should have loved to have been allowed to take it up."

fray, and the frustrating process had
to be repeated. From these duels
between the two air forces, the
strengths and weaknesses of the 'Emil',
compared with the Mark I versions of
the Spitfire and the Hurricane, quickly
became evident.

At altitudes above 20,000ft (6,000m),
the 'Emil' was slightly faster in level
flight and in the climb than the Spitfire.
At all altitudes, the German fighter was
much faster than the Hurricane. Below
15,000ft (4,600m), the Spitfire was the

Both the British Spitfire and the Hurricane could out-turn the Messerschmitt 109

---

faster in level flight. Both British fighter
types could out-turn the Me 109 at any
altitude. Me 109 pilots found the fuel
injection system fitted to the Daimler-
Benz 601 gave a useful advantage when
they had a Spitfire or a Hurricane on their
tail. The Messerschmitt pilot would push
down the nose of his fighter and 'bunt'
away from his purser. If an RAF fighter
attempted to follow the manoeuvre, the
negative 'G' shut off the fuel supply from
the float carburetter fitted to the Merlin
engine. There would be an ominous

Me 109 FRONT-LINE UNITS, 7 SEPTEMBER 1940

Unit	Aircraft total	Aircraft serviceable
Air Fleet 2 (Holland, Belgium, NE France)		
Fighter Geschwader 1		
Staff Flight	4	3 Pas de Calais area
Fighter Geschwader 3		
Staff Flight	3	3 Samer
I. Gruppe	23	14 Samer
II. Gruppe	24	21 Samer
III. Gruppe	25	23 Desvres
Fighter Geschwader 26		
Staff Flight	4	3 Audembert
I. Gruppe	27	20 Audembert
II. Gruppe	32	28 Marquise
III. Gruppe	29	26 Caffiers
Fighter Geschwader 27		
Staff Flight	5	4 Etaples
I. Gruppe	33	27 Etaples
II. Gruppe	37	33 Montreuil
III. Gruppe	31	27 Sempy
Fighter Geschwader 51		
Staff Flight	5	4 Saint Omer
I. Gruppe	36	33 Saint Omer, Saint Inglevert
II. Gruppe	22	13 Saint Omer, Saint Inglevert
III. Gruppe	44	31 Saint Omer
Fighter Geschwader 52		
Staff Flight	2	1 Laon/Couvron
I. Gruppe	21	7 Laon/Couvron
II. Gruppe	28	23 Pas de Calais area
III. Gruppe	31	16 Pas de Calais area
Fighter Geschwader 53		
Staff Flight	2	2 Pas de Calais area
II. Gruppe	33	24 Wissant
III. Gruppe	30	22 Pas de Calais area
Fighter Geschwader 54		
Staff Flight	4	2 Holland
I. Gruppe	28	23 Holland
II. Gruppe	35	27 Holland
III. Gruppe	28	23 Holland
Fighter Geschwader 77		
I. Gruppe	42	40 Pas de Calais area
Trials Gruppe 210	26	17 Denain (fighter-bomber unit, also flew Me 110s)
Air Fleet 3 (NW France)		
Fighter Geschwader 2		
Staff Flight	5	2 Beaumont-le-Roger
I. Gruppe	29	24 Beaumont-le-Roger
II. Gruppe	22	18 Beaumont-le-Roger
III. Gruppe	30	19 Le Havre Fighter
Geschwader 53		
I. Gruppe	34	27 Brittany area
Tactical Development (Lehr) Geschwader 2		
II. Gruppe	32	27 Saint Omer (fighter-bomber unit)
Air Fleet 5 (Norway)		
Fighter Geschwader 77		
II. Gruppe	44	35 Southern Norway

WAR DIARY OF 1ST GRUPPE OF FIGHTER GESCHWADER 3

Diary entry for 15 September 1940, now commemorated as Battle of Britain Day. At the time, this unit was part of Air Fleet 2, based at Samer near Boulogne under the command of Hauptmann Hans von Hahn.

"On 7 September the unit reported a strength of 23 Messerschmitt 109Es of which 14 were serviceable after four weeks of heavy fighting. 1200 [hours, take-off time] Escort (by 12 aircraft) of Do 17s against London. Obit Keller shot down a Spitfire, Leutnant Rohwer a Hurricane. Fw Wollmer dived into the Channel, the impact was seen by Lt Springer. This crash appears not to have been caused by enemy action. After a long dive Vollmer's machine rolled a quarter turn into a vertical dive and he did not succeed in bailing out. A motor boat detached from a German convoy near Cap Gris Nez and went to the scene of the crash. 1510 [hours] Operation by 9 aircraft to escort He 111s against London.

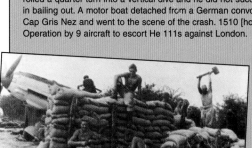

"At 1,500m there was almost total cloud cover. Over the Thames estuary and to the north of London there were gaps in the cloud. During the flight in there was contact with Spitfires. The bombers flew in loose formation to the north of London. Strong and accurate Flak. The Spitfires came from above, fired, and dived away. Hauptmann von Hahn shot down a Spitfire, Lt Rohwer probably destroyed a Hurricane. During an attack by Spitfires Oberleutnant Reumschuessel became separated from his wing man, Obfw Olejnik, and has not returned [this aircraft crashed near Charing, Kent; the pilot bailed out and was taken prisoner]. After he was separated from the formation Obfw Hessel was heard on the radio, but he failed to return [this aircraft crashed near Tenterden; the pilot bailed out and was taken prisoner]. Obfw Buchholz's aircraft was hit in the cooling system and forced down in the Channel. Obit Keller made contact with a rescue aircraft nearby, which picked up Buchholz. He had [minor] injuries and was taken to the military hospital at Boulogne. The body of Lt Kloiber has been washed ashore near St Cecile, and buried. Lt Meckel and 2 feldwebels attended the funeral. During the last few days news has been received from the Red Cross in Geneva that Obit Tiedmann, Obit Rau, Obit Loidolt, Lt Landry (these last two wounded) and Obfe Lamskemper have been captured by the British."

Scenes at the airfield at Caffiers near Calais, home of the Me 109 'Emils' of IIIrd Gruppe of Fighter Geschwader 26 during the Battle of Britain. The photos come from the personal album of Gerhard Schoepfel. *Top right:* Engine change of a fighter in the open. *Middle left:* Ground crewmen constructing a sandbag blast pen to protect a fighter on the ground. *Above left* and *middle right:* Aircraft in their camouflaged blast pens. *Right:* Officers of IIIrd Gruppe of Fighter Geschwader 26 discussing the next mission. Seated second from left is the unit commander, Major Adolf Galland. To his immediate left is Gerhard Schoepfel.

Above and right: 'Emils' loaded with 550lb bombs during attacks on England in the closing stages of the Battle of Britain.

warning splutter, and unless the RAF pilot restored positive 'G' immediately, his engine would stop dead. Several German pilots owed their survival to the Me 109's ability to bunt away from a pursuer.

■ RADIUS OF ACTION ■

While such marginal differences in performance and capability decided some actions during this critical period, it is important to view them in the overall context. Throughout the Battle of Britain, and particularly during its final phases when the capital was the target, the Me 109's limited radius of action was of crucial importance. During that contest, the Me 109, the Spitfire and the Hurricane each had an effective radius of action of about 100 miles (160km). For RAF fighters engaged in home defence operations, fighting over airfields where they could land to refuel, that distance

was adequate. However, for Me 109s flying in the bomber escort or support roles deep into enemy territory, it was inadequate. The German fighter pilots could not afford to spend long engaged in combat, their engines running at full throttle and guzzling fuel. If they were close to the limit of their radius of action, the Messerschmitts had to break off the action, often prematurely, and head for home. This factor greatly reduced the effectiveness of the German single-engined fighter force.

There is another point to consider. The cliché image of the Battle of Britain is that of a sky full of Me 109s, Spitfires and Hurricanes engaged in one-to-one turning fights with Me 109s. That might make for a spectacular painting or film shot, but it was far from the reality of air combat. Any pilot who fastened his attention too long on one enemy fighter ran the serious risk of setting himself up for a surprise attack by another.

PROVIDING CLOSE ESCORT FOR THE BOMBERS

"Sometimes we were ordered to provide close escort for a bomber formation, which I loathed. It gave the bomber crews the feeling they were being protected, and it might have deterred some of the enemy pilots. But for us fighter pilots it was very bad. We needed the advantages of altitude and speed so we could engage the enemy on favourable terms. As it was, the British fighters had the initiative of when and how to attack. The Heinkels cruised at about 4,000m [13,000ft] at about 300km/hr [190mph]. On close escort we flew at about 370km/hr [230mph], weaving from side to side to keep station on them. We needed to maintain speed, otherwise the Me 109s would have taken too long to accelerate to fighting speed if we were bounced by Spitfires. I hated having to fly direct escort. We had to stay with the bombers until our formation came under attack. When we saw the British fighters approaching we would want to accelerate to engage them. But our commander would call 'Everybody stay with the bombers.' We handed to the enemy the initiative of when and how they would attack us. Until they did we had to stay close to the bombers, otherwise their people would complain and there would be recriminations when we got back."

OBERLEUTNANT HANS SCHMOLLER-HALDY, ME 109 PILOT, FIGHTER GESCHWADER 54

Above: **At the end of the Battle of Britain, the top-scoring pilot in the Luftwaffe was Major Werner Moelders, the commander of Fighter Geschwader 51. On 22 October 1940 he scored his fiftieth aerial victory.**

On both sides, the really successful fighter pilots stalked their prey like hunters. They used the sun and cloud to remain unseen for as long as possible, as they edged into a favourable position before launching an attack. They then dived on their often unsuspecting prey, announcing their presence with a sudden and accurate burst of fire. There was no thought of chivalry. Usually the first thing the victim knew of the danger was when his aircraft shuddered under the impact of hits. A textbook example of this type of action appears in the Introduction to this book.

From the start of the Battle of Britain, one Gruppe operated the Me 109 in the fighter-bomber role, attacking targets in southern England. The fighter carried a bomb load of up to 550lb (249kg). In the final part of the Battle, from the end of September, several Me 109 units flew aircraft modified for the fighter-bomber role. The defending fighters found the fast, high-flying German fighter-bombers difficult targets to engage. As a result, the latter suffered minimal losses. On the other hand, the Me 109 carried only a small weight of bombs, and their scattered bombing meant that the attacks had only nuisance value.

■ REPUTATION INTACT ■

The Me 109 force emerged from the Battle of Britain with its reputation still intact. True, it had suffered losses at the hands of the RAF pilots. But during these hard-fought engagements, the Me 109 force had usually dealt out blows at least as hard as those it took.

Alongside the Spitfire Mark I, the 'Emil' was still a contender for the title of most effective fighter plane in the world. The new variant of the German fighter about to enter service, the Me 109 'Friedrich', would be even better.

Left: **Hauptmann Horst Tietzen, the commander of 5th Staffel of Fighter Geschwader 51, with his personal 'Emil' with 18 victory bars on the tail. On the afternoon of 18 August 1940, when his victory score stood at 20, he was shot down and killed during an action with Hurricanes of No. 501 Squadron.**

"THE MOST SERIOUS AND UNPARDONABLE ERROR"

"On 23 September our mission was a free huntng sweep in the triangle Ramsgate–Canterbury–Folkestone, where British fighter activity had been reported. With three of my pilots I took off at 10.27 and headed towards Ramsgate in a slow climb to 4,500m [about 15,000ft]. The weather was strange, with layers of cloud in which aircraft could easily hide. There were several flights of aircraft about which we saw for a moment before they disappeared, we never knew if they were British or German. It was uncanny. We flew in wide curves, always changing altitude, never flying straight for long. We had been flying for 60 minutes, I thought that was enough and we were turning for home when I suddenly observed a Hurricane squadron between Ramsgate and Dover, 12 aircraft in four 'pulks' flying one behind the other. They were about 1,000m (2,873ft) below us and climbing in wide curves, like a creeping worm. My impression was that it was a Hurricane squadron on a training mission. The Hurricane pilots had no idea that four 109s were above them following each of their movements, like an eagle looking down on its prey. The spectacle was so fascinating that we completely forgot what was going on around us. That is the most serious and unpardonable error a fighter pilot can commit, and catastrophe immediately followed. Four Spitfires, of which we had been unaware due to our carelessness, attacked us from out of the sun. They fired at us from behind, roared close over our heads at high speed and disappeared back into the sky. As we broke formation fearing another attack from the Spitfires, I saw a 109 going down in flames on my right. It was Oberfeldwebel Knipscher, we never heard what happened to him."

OBERLEUTNANT HANS SCHMOLLER-HALDY, ME 109 PILOT, FIGHTER GESCHWADER 54

Top: An 'Emil' crash-landed on a French beach. During the Battle of Britain, this fighter was not fitted with drop tanks, and lacked the range to penetrate far into southern England. Several were lost when they ran out of fuel on their way home following air combats or after encountering strong headwinds.

Above: Me 109E-7s of Fighter Geschwader 1, a unit that spent most of the war operating in the defence of the German homeland. (via Obert)

Right: Major Adolf Galland climbing out of the cockpit of his 'Emil' after a sortie over England during the Battle of Britain.

ENTER THE 'FRIEDRICH'

During 1940, the Messerschmitt company initiated a programme to clean up the airframe of the Me 109 and improve its fighting capability. The new variant became the Me 109 'Friedrich'. Compared with the 'Emil', the more obvious external changes were the more rounded spinner and nose contours, the rounded wing tips and the partially retractable tail wheel. The main production version was fitted with the new Mauser 15mm cannon, one of which fired through the propeller hub. This weapon had nearly twice the firing rate of the older 20mm Oerlikon cannon, and its far higher muzzle velocity made it a much more effective weapon than its predecessor.

Luftwaffe pilots who flew the 'Friedrich' remembered this variant with affection. It was faster than the 'Emil' and it handled rather better in the air. It was, in the truest sense of the expression, a 'fighter pilot's fighter'. The 'Freidrich' entered service in the spring of 1941, and by the middle of the year two-thirds of the Luftwaffe fighter force flew this type. Also at this time, the Royal Air Force introduced the Mark V Spitfire into its home defence squadrons, a move that restored the balance between the fighter forces of the two sides.

■ NORTH AFRICA ■

That balance existed only over north-west Europe, however. Until the spring

Top: A brand new Me 109 'Friedrich' in factory markings shows off its distinctive rounded wing form above the Alps.
Above: A 'Friedrich' of Fighter Geschwader 26 returning to its base at Liegescourt in northern France in the summer of 1941. (Schoepfel)
Opposite: Two 'Emils' of Fighter Geschwader 27 on patrol over the North African desert.

MESSERSCHMITT 109 F-2

Type Single-seat general-purpose fighter

Armament One Mauser 15mm cannon firing through the propeller spinner (200 rounds); two Rheinmetall-Borsig 7.9mm MGs synchronized to fire through airscrew (500 rounds per gun)

Power plant One Daimler-Benz DB 601N inverted V-12 liquid-cooled engine developing 1,200hp for take-off

Dimensions Span 32ft 6in (9.92m); length 29ft 4in (8.94m)

Weight Normal operational take-off 6,174lb (2,800kg)

Performance Maximum speed 373mph at 19,700ft (600km/hr at 6,000m); service ceiling 36,100ft (11,000m)

Top: 'Friedrich' wearing the personal markings of the commander of IIIrd Gruppe of Fighter Geschwader 2 based in northern France, photographed in 1941.
Above: An Me 109F of Fighter Geschwader 26 outside its camouflaged dispersal hangar in northern France.

of 1942, the Spitfire fighter units operated only from bases in Great Britain. Meanwhile, units equipped with the 'Friedrich' were heavily involved in the campaigns in North Africa and the Soviet Union, where the new fighter easily outflew the less modern types opposing it. For the German fighter pilots, this was a 'happy time' when many of them amassed large victory scores.

The foremost successful 'Friedrich' fighter pilot was Leutnant Hans-Joachim Marseille. He gained seven victories during the Battle of Britain while flying the 'Emil' before moving to the North African theatre to join Fighter Geschwader 27. From the beginning of

ATTACK ON RUSSIA

During the weeks following the invasion of Russia, packs of German fighters ranged far and wide over enemy territory. Close to the ground, the Polikarpov I-16, the main Soviet fighter type, was almost as fast as the Me 109F that equipped the majority of Luftwaffe fighter units. But the Type 24's radial engine was optimized for low-altitude operations, and as height increased its performance fell away steadily; at 20,000ft (6,096m) the I-16 was about 100mph (160km/hr) slower than the German fighter. Although the Soviet fighters were more manoeuvrable than their adversaries, in a fighter-versus-fighter combat that advantage did no more than allow a pilot to avoid being shot down, provided he saw his attacker in good time. For the most part, the Soviet fighter pilots had to dance to their enemies' tune. Typical of the scrappy actions taking place that morning was one near Brest-Litovsk, described by Unteroffizier Reibel of 1st Gruppe of Fighter Geschwader 53: "I was flying as wing man to Lt Zellot. We flew in the direction of Brest from Labinka. As my leader ordered a turn about, I saw two biplanes in front of us. I immediately reported them and we brought them under attack. When we were about 200m [61ft] from them they both pulled into a tight turn to the right. We pulled up high and then began a new attack, but though we both opened fire it was without success. Soon there were about ten other [enemy] machines in the area. My leader ran in to attack one of the planes while I remained high in order to cover him. Then an I-15 became separated from the others. I immediately prepared to attack it, but I had to break away when another enemy machine, which I had not seen, suddenly appeared 50m [15ft] in front of me. I opened fire with machine-guns and the cannon and it burst into flames and spun out of control. Apparently the pilot had baled out. Then I had to turn away, as I had two [enemy] machines behind me." Using their superior speed, the German fighters easily pulled away.

Above: Me 109 'Emils' of Fighter Geschwader 52 pictured at Kabaracie, Rumania, in the spring of 1941, shortly before the attack on the Soviet Union. The 'snake' marking on the rear fuselage indicated that these aircraft belonged to the IIIrd Gruppe.

Left: Me 109 'Emil' fighter-bomber of Fighter Geschwader 54 operating over the Eastern Front in 1942.
Middle: Me 109 'Friedrich' of Fighter Geschwader 54 pictured beside a captured Soviet I-16 fighter. The more powerful and cleaner-lined German fighter had a considerable speed advantage over its enemy counterpart, especially at high altitude.
Bottom: Me 109 'Friedrich' of Fighter Geschwader 53, with the unit's 'Ace of Spades' insignia on the cowling, at a forward airfield in the Leningrad sector on the Eastern Front during the winter of 1941–2.

1942, his victory total rose rapidly. With no Spitfires yet operating in that area, the 'Friedrich' was superior to the Hurricane and Tomahawk fighters flown by the RAF and its allies. During a remarkable action on 3 June 1942, Marseille shot down six Tomahawks in rapid succession. The action is well documented and the combat is confirmed in the records of the victim unit, No. 5 Squadron South African Air Force. By the time of his death in September 1942, Marseille's tally of 'kills' stood at 158.

Early on, the 15mm cannon fitted to the 'Friedrich' was replaced with a fast-firing 20mm Mauser cannon. With the two machine-guns mounted above the engine cowling, the closely grouped weapons gave

Me 109s IN NORTH AFRICA

Opposite:

. Hauptmann Karl-Wolfgang Redlich of 1st Gruppe Fighter Geschwader 27 (left, holding papers), briefing pilots before taking off from Catania in Sicily to fly to North Africa. The 'Emil' in the background is fitted with a dust filter over the engine air intake. (Schroer)

. Ground-running an 'Emil' at Catania, to warm the engine before setting out for North Africa. (Schroer)

. Me 109 'Emils' of Fighter Geschwader 27 dispersed around the forward landing ground at Gambut in Libya. The photograph gives a good impression of the primitive conditions under which the unit had to operate. (Schroer)

. Ground crewmen turning the handle for the inertia starter of the Daimler-Benz 601 engine. The handle rotated a heavy flywheel which, when it was turning fast enough, was clutched to the engine to turn it over and start it.

. 'Emils' of Fighter Geschwader 27 on patrol over the desert.

. Me 109F of Fighter Geschwader 27 preparing to get airborne. Note that this aircraft is missing its spinner.

. Hauptmann Hans-Joachim Marseille of Fighter Geschwader 27, the most successful German fighter pilot in North Africa. At the time of his death in September 1942, his victory score stood at 158.

. Fighter ace Leutnant Werner Schroer, Adjutant of IInd Gruppe of Fighter Geschwader 27, with his personal aircraft. At the end of the war, his victory score stood at 114. (Schroer)

dense pattern of fire that proved very effective against enemy fighters and light bombers. Against the four-engined bombers, with their tougher structures, it was another matter however.

■ FIRE POWER ■

From mid-1942, the Me 109F units operating over western Europe and North Africa encountered the American B-17 Flying Fortress and B-24 Liberator heavy bombers with increasing frequency. On average, it needed about 20 hits with 20mm rounds to knock down one of these rugged aircraft. When in formation, the heavy bombers put up a powerful defensive cross-fire which forced the fighters to make high-speed firing

passes. Under those conditions, only an exceptionally good shot could achieve the required number of hits using a single cannon.

Greater fire power was needed, and in answer to this problem the 'Friedrich' was modified to carry a blister under each wing containing an extra 20mm cannon and ammunition. The change trebled the fighter's fire power, but at no small cost in terms of its performance and general handling. It was the first ominous sign of a problem that would afflict the Me 109 and other German piston-engined fighter types for the remainder

Above: 'Friedrich' of Fighter Geschwader 77 operating on the Leningrad front in 1942. (Pichler via Obert)

of the war. In short, any fighter that had sufficient fire power to engage Allied heavy bombers successfully would be too heavy and too unwieldy to engage Allied fighters on equal terms.

That critical shortcoming would become all too evident when the next variant of the fighter enered production, the 'Gustav', which is described in the next chapter.

EASY TIMES IN RUSSIA

Initially, the German fighter pilots had an easy time over Russia, and the more talented of them built up huge victories scores. There were plenty of opportunities for everyone, however, even the inexperienced pilots. In the summer of 1942, Unteroffizier Walther Hagenah was posted from training to 1st Gruppe of Fighter Geschwader 3 operating the Me 109F. He flew as wing man to Oberfeldwebel Otto Wessling, a skilful and experienced pilot. Hagenah told this author: "Wessling was a superb leader who seemed to be able to score hits from ranges as great as 400m [1,312ft]. He would manoeuvre into a position of advantage above his prey, dive on his prey and open fire from long range, hit his enemy and pull away without getting close to his foe. My first weeks as an operational fighter pilot were a disappointment. To be sure I fired at enemy aircraft, but all I seemed to hit was the air. I was beginning to get discouraged. One day Wessling took me to one side on the ground and said, 'Now it is time that you made your first victory!' On 12 August 1942, we were on patrol on the central Russian front and he spotted a pair of LAGG-3 fighters. He took us round into an attacking position on their tails and down we went. We came from out of the sun and achieved surprise. He hit one of them from about 400m [1,312ft] and down it went. Then he called me and said, 'Now you go ahead and hit the other one!' But the second Russian pilot had a lot of pluck and he really threw his aircraft about the sky in an effort to shake us off his tail. Then Wessling joined in the dogfight, but at the same time telling me what I had to do to get 'my' kill. Eventually he succeeded in manoeuvring both me and the Russian fighter into a position where I could open fire at it – just as a gamekeeper will chase a deer into a position where a wealthy man can hit it with his gun. All I had to do was follow Wessling's instructions and fire when he said, and I hit the enemy fighter. So I achieved my victory. I was very proud. Wessling was big enough to keep quiet about how I got it."

During the Second World War, the principal fighter types in the major warring nations underwent courses of development to improve their fighting capability. They were fitted with more powerful (and heavier) engines, more effective (and heavier) armament, larger (and heavier) fuel tankage and additional (and heavier) protective armour and items of equipment.

As the fighter steadily gained weight, from time the airframe had to be stiffened to restore its original strength factors. That added a further twist to the spiral of increasing weight. Since the fighter's wing area usually remained constant, each increase in weight led to increase in wing loading. And that, inevitably, led to a deterioration in the fighter's handling characteristics. Stalling speeds became higher, control forces heavier, turning performance worsened and, in many cases, the aircraft developed vicious traits.

No fighter design suffered more from this remorseless process than the Me 109. Even at the start of the war, it will be remembered, the Me 109 had already passed through several variants. By the spring of 1942, it had reached the end of its effective development, and ideally it should then have passed out of production. However, Messerschmitt's planned replacement fighter, the Me 209, was still on the drawing board.

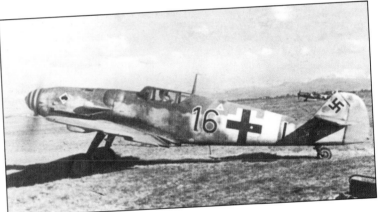

The Me 109G-2 was 660 pounds heavier than its predecessor, the Me 109F

At that time, the war was still going well for Germany. Her leaders confidently expected that the campaign on the Eastern front would come to a victorious end in the autumn of 1942. Until a replacement fighter type was ready, the Luftwaffe opted to squeeze a little more speed from the Me 109 and keep the fighter in full production.

The new variant, the Me 109 'Gustav', was designed around the Daimler-Benz 605 engine. In essence, this was a DB 601 with the cylinder block rebored to increase the engine's capacity from 33.9 litres to 35.7 litres. The additional capacity gave an extra 175 horse power at full throttle, for no significant increase in the engine's external dimensions. That fact did not prevent the new variant of the Me 109 from putting on weight, however. The first major production version, the 'Gustav-2', was 660lb (300kg) or about 10 per cent heavier than the earlier 'Friedrich' and its handling charac-

Top: Me 109 'Gustav' of Fighter Geschwader 54 pictured at a forward airfield in Russia, showing the difficult conditions encountered during the spring thaw.
Above: Me 109 'Gustav' of Fighter Geschwader 53 pictured at a forward airfield in Sicily in 1943. (via Rigglesford)
Opposite: Pilots of Fighter Geschwader 53 at readiness snatching a quick meal beside one of their aircraft. (via Schliephake)

istics were correspondingly worse; compared with the Me 109 'Berta', the figures were 2,200lb (1,000kg) and 46 per cent respectively! During May 1942, a total of 234 Me 109s came off the production lines in Germany and Austria, most of them 'Gustavs'.

MESSERSCHMITT 109 G-2

Type Single-seat general-purpose fighter

Armament One Mauser 20mm cannon firing through the spinner (150 rounds);
two Rheinmetall-Borsig 7.9mm MGs synchronized to fire through the airscrew
(500 rounds per gun)

Power plant One Daimler-Benz DB 605A inverted V-12 liquid-cooled engine
developing 1,475hp for take-off

Dimensions Span 32ft 6in (9.92m); length 29ft 0in (8.85m)

Weight Normal operational take-off 6,832lb (3,100kg)

Performance Maximum speed 406mph at 28,535ft (654km/hr at 8,700m);
service ceiling 39,360ft (12,000m)

Soon after the 'Gustav' entered service with Fighter Geschwader 27, Hans-Joachim Marseille lost his life while flying the type. In September 1942, his victory score passed the 150 mark, making him the first fighter ace in history to achieve this total. On the final day of the month he flew a newly delivered 'Gustav-2' on a bomber escort mission over Egypt. There was no contact with the enemy and the flight was uneventful, until on the return flight the aircraft's engine started to smoke. Then it caught fire. The cockpit filled with fumes and, escorted by his comrades, Marseille stayed with the aircraft until he reached German-held territory. Then he jumped from the stricken fighter, but his luck had deserted him. As he left the Messerschmitt, it appears that his head struck some part of its structure and he was knocked unconscious. His parachute did not open and he was killed on hitting the ground. Subsequent examination of his parachute revealed that it was still in the pack, held closed by the ripcord which had not been pulled.

Marseille jumped from his aircraft, but for once luck had deserted him

Small numbers of 'Gustav-2s' were modified for the tactical reconnaissance role, with the cannon removed and a vertical camera mounted in the rear fuselage. The use of the Me 109 (and also the

FW 190) for this purpose became necessary because the increasing enemy fighter opposition on each of the battle fronts meant that slower reconnaissance types incurred heavy losses. Modified versions of each of the new main variants of the Me 109 would be used for tactical reconnaissance for the remainder of the war.

The next major production version of the fighter, the 'Gustav-6', started to leave the assembly lines in the autumn

of 1942. This differed from the G-2 in that it carried two 13mm heavy machine-guns on top of the engine cowling, in place of the earlier rifle-calibre weapons. To cover the larger breech mechanism of the 13mm guns, the fighter had two large bulges on the cowling in front of the windscreen.

■ 210mm ROCKETS ■

The Luftwaffe issued a range of field modification kits to allow units to 'customize' the new fighter for specific operational roles. The R-1 kit, for example, provided an under-fuselage rack to carry a single bomb weighing up to 550lb (249kg). The R-2 kit provided for a tubular launcher under each wing to carry a 210mm rocket, for use against enemy bomber formations or ground targets. The R-4 kit provided a blister mounting for a 30mm heavy cannon and ammunition, one to fit under either wing.

'WILD BOAR'
MESSERSCHMITT 109s

Above: Me 109G-2s operating in the 'Wild Boar' single-engine night-fighter role to counter RAF bomber attacks, summer 1943.

From mid-1943, the Luftwaffe began to employ small numbers of single-engined fighters, including Me 109s, to engage RAF night bombers attacking cities in Germany. Over the target, the concentrations of searchlights, the fires on the ground and the Pathfinders' marker flares often combined to illuminate the bombers. The single-seaters patrolling high above the target could then make visual attacks on the raiders. To prevent conflict with the flak defences, it was agreed that the latter would engage bombers flying below a certain altitude, typically 18,000ft (5,500m). Above that altitude, the fighters would engage bombers. The single-engined night fighter tactics bore the apt title 'Wild Boar'. For the remainder of the war, these methods were an integral part of the German night air defence system.

WEAPONS INSTALLATION FITTED TO Me 109G-5 AND G-6

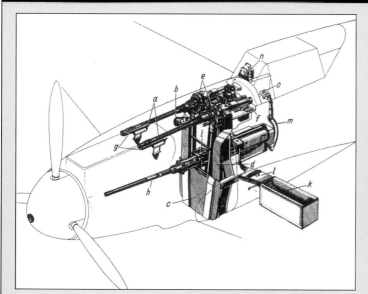

KEY:

a. MG 131 13mm heavy machine-guns

b. Electrical synchronization unit for firing MG 131s through the airscrew disc

c. Magazine for MG 131 ammunition

d. Empty case chute for port MG 131

e. Mountings for MG 131s

f. Ignition coil, to provide high voltage for electrically fired MG 131 ammunition

g. Mounting brackets for nose fairing

h. MG 151 20mm cannon firing through propeller spinner

i. Front mounting of MG 151

k. Magazine for MG 151 ammunition

l. Feed chute for MG 151 ammunition

m. Control column, with firing button for weapons

n. Revi 16B reflector sight

o. Arming switch for weapons

Also, the 'Gustav-6' had provision to carry one or two separate power-boosting systems, to inject a fluid into the supercharger of the DB 605 engine. To boost power at altitudes above 20,000ft (6,096m), the GM-1 system injected nitrous oxide (laughing gas) into the engine. The nitrous oxide was held in liquid form in a heavily lagged pressurized container in the rear fuselage, and the complete system weighed 670lb (304kg). To boost power

Above: Diagram from an official Luftwaffe handbook, showing the fuselage armament fitted as standard to Me 109 Gustav-5 and Gustav-6. These fighters had a 20mm Mauser cannon firing through the airscrew hub, and two 13mm Rheinmetall-Borsig heavy machine-guns above the engine cowling synchronized to fire through the airscrew. On some later aircraft, the engine-mounted cannon was replaced by a Rheinmetall-Borsig 30mm weapon.

Below: The 'Gustav' did not suffer fools gladly. If the pilot opened the throttle too quickly during take-off, the powerful engine torque was liable to lift the fighter off the ground before it attained flying speed. Often the fighter rolled upside down and smashed on the ground under full power, giving the pilot little chance of escape. (Schliephake)

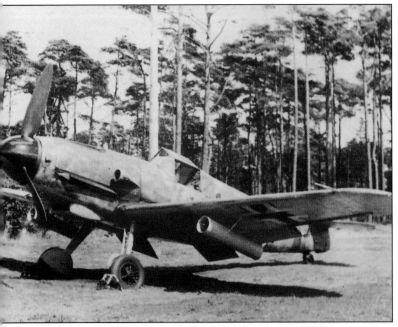

orated. On each battle front in turn the Luftwaffe was thrown on the defensive. More and more fighters were required, and the 'Gustav', originally introduced as a stopgap type, was built in ever-greater numbers. During 1943, production of the Me 109 was twice than in the previous year, with more than 6,400 'Gustavs' delivered to the Luftwaffe.

One factor that led to demands for increasing numbers of air defence fighters was the daylight attacks by US heavy bombers on targets in Germany. What had started as infrequent raids by a few dozen bombers against fringe targets had grown into deep penetration attacks by several hundred bombers able to inflict severe devastation. To meet the new threat, several fighter Gruppen were withdrawn from the battle fronts to bolster the defences of the homeland.

In the summer of 1943, Unteroffizier Hans Seyringer was posted to IInd Gruppe of Fighter Geschwader 27, a day

The young pilot had only about 200 flying hours in his logbook

fighter unit based at Wiesbaden and equipped with the 'Gustav-6'. The young pilot had come straight from training and had only about 200 flying hours in his logbook. His recollections give a good impression of what it was like to serve with such a unit.

During bomber-interception missions the fighters usually carried a 66 gallon (300 litre) drop tank under the fuselage. The standard armament fitted to 'Gustavs' on Seyringer's unit was three 20mm cannon and two 13mm machine-guns. Some of the aircraft also carried two 210mm rocket launchers under the wings, though as an inexperienced pilot Seyringer never flew with these weapons.

When waiting on the ground at readiness, the aircraft were usually drawn up by Staffeln in line abreast. The four Staffeln, each with about a dozen 'Gustav-6s', were dispersed separately at 90-degree intervals around the perimeter of the grass airfield. Once the pilots had

Top: Me 109 'Gustav-2s' belonging to a tactical reconnaissance Gruppe. This version had the nose-mounted cannon removed, and a vertical camera fitted in the fuselage immediately behind the cockpit.
Above: Me 109 'Gustav-2' of Fighter Geschwader 11 at Jever during 1943, fitted with underwing launchers for two 210mm air-to-air rockets for use against US heavy bomber formations.

at altitudes below 20,000ft, the MW system injected a water/methanol mixture into the engine (the water cooled the charge and provided the extra power, and the methanol prevented the water from freezing at high altitude). The complete MW system weighed 300lb (136kg).

As the 'Gustav-6' entered service, Germany's war fortunes suddenly deteri-

Above: A close-up of the rocket installation on a 'Gustav'.

Left: Me 109 'Gustav' of the Finnish Air Force. The type entered that service in March 1943 and remained in use until 1954.

the opposite direction accidentally loosed off a couple of rockets. The missiles came scorching past Seyringer's Staffel just as the fighters were getting airborne. Their proximity caused considerable consternation but, fortunately for the pilots involed, no damage!

■ TACTICS ■

Once the ground controller had brought a fighter Gruppe within visual range of an enemy formation, the Gruppe leader decided on the type of attack to employ. Usually Seyringer's Gruppe attacked bombers from the rear, the fighters flying in four-aircraft units in line abreast or line astern. After their initial attack, the fighters split into pairs to make further firing runs. Sometimes Seyringer's Gruppe made head-on attacks, though he did not like this method. He felt that the time spent manoeuvring into position for such an attack was out of proportion to the very short firing pass that resulted.

een brought to cockpit readiness, the rder to scramble was given by firing a reen flare from the control tower. From hen on, it was important to get the Gruppe into the air and assembled into attle formation as rapidly as possible. To chieve this, two of the Staffeln on pposite sides of the airfield began simulaneous take-off runs, moving on parallel eadings separated by a few hundred ards. As the first two Staffeln passed ach other at the centre of the airfield, the ther two Staffeln began their take-off ns also heading in opposite directions.

After take-off, the leader orbited once over the airfield so the individual Staffeln could start to move into position behind him. Then he turned on to his intercept heading and began a slow climb away. Once the formation was fully assembled, he increased his rate of climb.

These tactics provided the most rapid means of getting a Gruppe into the air and assembled into formation. There was little small margin for safety if anything went wrong, however. Seyringer recalled a nerve-racking incident when, due to incorrect fitting, a fighter taking off in

Above: 'Gustav-6' carrying the white fuselage band and wing tips of a unit operating on the Mediterranean front.
Right: Unteroffizier Hans Seyringer of Fighter Geschwader 27, whose experiences are described in the text, pictured with his 'Gustav-6'. With a victory score of four enemy aircraft destroyed, he was shot down and wounded during an engagement with American escort fighters in February 1944. (Seyringer)

Until late in 1943, the American escort fighters lacked the range to penetrate deep into Germany. Serringer's unit had few encounters with them and he thought that was as well, for a heavily laden 'Gustav-6' was no match for a Thunderbolt.

To Hans Seyringer, the effect of the fighter's extensive development process on handling was all too evident. To put it simply, the 'Gustav' was too heavy and its engine too powerful for the fighter's small wing and tail surfaces. When carrying a full armament and drop tank, the aircraft required careful handling during take-off. If there was heavy-handedness of the controls, the fighter was liable to react viciously. If, for example, the pilot opened the throttle too quickly, the powerful engine torque was liable to lift the fighter off the ground before it attained flying speed. The 'Gustav' would drop its left wing, roll on its back and smash into the ground, giving the pilot little chance of escape. The 'Gustav' did not suffer fools gladly.

During 1943, the Luftwaffe tactics to counter the American heavy bomber raids were in a continual state of development. Home defence units used any type of weapon that came to hand. Fighter Geschwader 11 carried out experiments in air-to-air bombing, using

DISASTER FOR THE GERMAN DAY FIGHTER FORCE

In the spring of 1944, the American escort fighters were able to reach almost every part of Germany. The new Mustang was superior in performance to the Me 109, and it was usually present in greater numbers. As a result, the German day fighter units took increasingly heavy losses. At the end of April 1944, Generalmajor Adolf Galland reported: "Between January and April 1944 our day fighter arm lost more than 1,000 pilots. They included our best Staffel, Gruppe and Geschwader commanders. The time has come when our force is within sight of collapse." Now the German pilots had to fight for their very survival, and one by one even the best of them were being picked off. Gone were the days when the aces could 'play' enemy planes to allow their less experienced colleagues to get easy kills, as they did over Russia a couple of years earlier. One of those who died in action with the American fighters in April 1944 was Leutnant Otto Wessling, then credited with 83 victories, who had set up Walther Hagenah's first 'kill' described earlier.

time-fused 550lb (249kg) released from above the bomber formation. Initially, it seemed this tactic might have a good chance of success. Even if the bombs did not destroy the enemy planes, they might damage some of them sufficiently to force them to leave their formation. Other fighters could then finish off the wounded birds as easy prey. There were serious problems with this method, however. Carrying a bomb in place of a drop tank, the 'Gustav' had a short radius of action. Also, it proved difficult to vector the heavily laden fighter into position above a high-flying bomber formation. Moreover, since there was no effective proximity fuse then available, the problem of getting the bomb to

MESSERSCHMITT 109 G-2 VERSUS HAWKER TEMPEST

At the beginning of 1944, a captured Me 109 'Gustav-2' was flown in a comparative trial against the latest RAF fighter type, the Hawker Tempest Mark V. These extracts from the official report show that the German fighter was outclassed in almost every respect.

"**Maximum speed:** The Tempest possesses an advantage of 40–50mph [64–80km/hr] at heights below 20,000ft [5,850m] but at heights in excess of 20,000ft [6,096m] the advantage possessed by the Tempest rapidly diminishes. **Climb:** The climb of the Me 109 is superior to that of the Tempest at all heights but this advantage is not pronounced at heights below 5,000ft [1,520m]. When both the aircraft commence a dive at the same speed and are put into climbing attitude, the Tempest is slightly superior, but providing the Tempest possesses the initial advantage in speed, it has no difficulty in holding it providing the speed is kept in excess of 250mph [400km/hr]. **Dive:** Comparative dives between these aircraft show that the Tempest will pull away from the Me 109. This is not so marked in the early stages of the dive, but in a prolonged descent the Tempest is greatly superior. **Turning circle:** It was found that in this aspect of manoeuvrability the Tempest was slightly superior to the Me 109. **Rate of roll:** At speeds below 350 IAS [mph indicated, 564km/hr] there is practically nothing to choose between the two aircraft, but when this speed is exceeded the Tempest can out-manoeuvre the Me 109 by making a quick change of bank and direction. **Conclusions:** In the attack the Tempest can always follow the Me 109, except in a slow steep climb. In the combat area the Tempest should maintain a high speed, and in defence may do anything except attempt a climb at low speed."

Below: Comparative trials revealed that the Hawker Tempest Mark V, which entered service in the RAF early in 1944, was superior to the Me 109 'Gustav-2' in almost every respect.

detonate as it passed the target aircraft defied solution. Most of the bombs detonated well clear of their intended victims, and after a month or so the unit abandoned this form of attack.

During the spring of 1944, following the introduction of new and larger drop tanks, the American escort fighters were able to reach almost every part of Germany. The new Mustang fighters were superior in performance to the defending Me 109s, Me 110s, Me 410s and FW 190s. Moreover, the escort fighters operated in large numbers, and as a result the German fighter units took heavy losses.

■ HOME DEFENCE ■

By now the greater part of the Luftwaffe fighter force was committed in the defence of the homeland. And it was losing pilots faster than the German flying training schools could provide replacements. The Luftwaffe was being bled white. The only possibility of reversing this trend was with the large-scale deployment of the Messerschmitt 262 jet fighter. Yet this type was still not ready to enter mass production (see next section of this book).

Although the 'Gustav' was now well beyond its effective development life, new sub-types continued to appear. By optimizing it for a narrow range of combat roles, the fighter might survive in action. Thus, the 'Gustav-10', for example, was built specifically to engage in high-altitude fighter-versus-fighter combat. These aircraft carried the new Daimler-Benz 605D engine with an

enlarged supercharger and the GM-1 power boosting. Their armament was reduced to one 20mm cannon and two 13mm machine-guns. They were assigned to units whose task was to provide top cover for more heavily armed fighters delivering attacks on bomber formations. In addition, small numbers of 'Gustav-10s' were modified for the tactical reconnaissance role, with the two heavy machine-guns removed and a fixed vertical camera mounted in the rear fuselage.

■ A DESPERATE TIME ■

In the spring of 1944, the German aircraft industry underwent a major reorganization. The Luftwaffe,

Above: Damaged Me 109 'Gustav' trailing glycol smoke after being hit in the cooling system during an engagement with a US escort fighter. Soon after this picture was taken, the 'Gustav' was shot down. (USAF)
Below: Me 109G-6s of IIIrd Gruppe Fighter Geschwader 27 waiting at readiness at Wiesbaden-Erbenheim in 1944. The broad red band around the rear fuselage indicated that the aircraft belonged to a Reich air defence unit. (Schroer)

IN ACTION DURING THE
FINAL MONTHS OF THE WAR

Leutnant Hans-Ulrich Flade flew the Me 109 'Gustav' and the 'Kurfurst' with IInd Gruppe of Fighter Geschwader 27 early in 1945. In previous months, the production of these fighters had reached an all-time high, and if an aircraft was damaged it was usually simpler to get a new fighter than repair the old one: "We simply went to the depot nearby, where they had hundreds of brand new 109s – G-10s, G-14s and even the very latest K models. There was no proper organization any more; the depot staff just said, 'There are the aircraft, take what you want and go away.'" But getting fuel, that was more difficult. Flade's Gruppe had a strength of about 20 pilots, but it was losing these at a rate of two or three each day. Morale on the unit was low. "Each morning we pilots had breakfast together, and the replacements would come in. The older pilots regarded the newcomers as though they had only days to live – and with reason, for the standard of fighter conversion training was now so low that most of the new pilots flew only two or three missions before they were shot down. I remember many conversations along these lines – not exactly a cheerful subject for a young man who had just joined his first operational unit!" The Gruppe operated in the top-cover role, to keep the American escort fighters off the backs of other German fighters making for the bombers. "We followed the old rules: dive as a pair or a four out of the sun, make a quick attack to break up their formation and make them drop their tanks, then climb out of danger and assess the situation. If conditions were favourable, we would go down for a second attack. Always the escorts were so numerous that it would have been foolish to get into a dogfight."

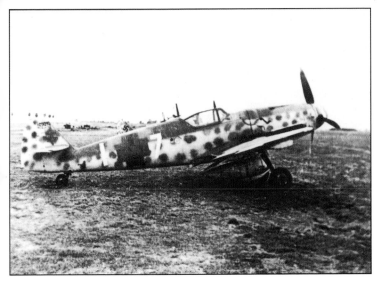

Left: The Me 109G-14 featured a larger rudder and a redesigned cockpit canopy to give better vision to the sides and the rear. This example belonged to IIIrd Gruppe of Fighter Geschwader 3, a unit that flew escort missions for more heavily armoured fighters delivering attacks on US heavy bomber formations. (Romm)

Below: Me 109 'Kurfurst', the final version of the fighter to go into production in Germany before the end of the war. As well as the revised tail surfaces and redesigned canopy fitted to the late production 'Gustavs', this variant featured a more powerful Daimler-Benz 605 engine and carried two 15mm cannons mounted on top of the engine.

by this time in a desperate situation, needed every modern fighter it could lay its hands on. Under the new Luftwaffe procurement plan, almost the entire capacity of the industry was turned over to the manufacture of fighter-type aircraft. At the same time, to render the industry less vulnerable to air attack, a large part of the aircraft construction and assembly work was dispersed into small factories and workshops dotted throughout the country.

Once the new system was in place, production of the Me 109 rose in leaps and bounds, despite the heavy and continual raids on German cities and industrial centres. For the Me 109, September 1944 was the peak month, with the Luftwaffe taking delivery of

Above and left: The unusual 'Mistel' weapon, an Me 109F mounted rigidly on top of a Junkers 88 bomber that had the cabin removed and a large warhead fitted in its place. The Me 109 pilot aligned the bomber on the target, then fired explosive bolts to separate his aircraft so that he could make his escape.
Below: The Avia S.199 was manufactured in Czechoslovakia after the war, using components for the Me 109 'Gustav' built in that country. The fighter was fitted with a Jumo 211 engine, which gave the unusual nose contours. (Hurt)

1,605 new aircraft. That year, 14,212 examples of this type of aircraft were delivered, more than twice as many as in the previous year, which had itself been a record. At this stage of the war, the units equipped with Me 109s always had plenty of aircraft, although there were worsening shortages of trained pilots and fuel as the tide turned inexorably against the German forces.

Despite the known poor handling qualities of the Me 109 'Gustav', work continued in attempts to squeeze yet more speed and combat capability out of the basic design. The final variant of the Me 109 to enter large-scale production was the 'Kurfurst', deliveries of which began at the end of September 1944.

Above: The wreckage of a Messerchmitt after being brought down by enemy fire.
Left: The Messerchmitt in flight.

Left: Messerschmitt Bf 109G-6/U2 (TP814 c/n 412951) RAF, possibly photographed at Air Fighting Development Unit, Duxford, England, UK, 1941–2. (Courtesy of Gladwin-Simms Collection via ww.1000aircraftphotos.com)

Above: A row of Messerschmitt Bf 109 Luftwaffes.
(Courtesy of Alfarrabista German Press Photos Collection)

Below: Messerschmitt Bf 109E-3 (AE479 c/n 1304) RAF.
This photo was possibly taken during a flight from
Duxford, Cambridgeshire, England, UK, in 1941 after
a new tail unit and a later-type canopy had been fitted,
following an accident at the Aeroplane and Armament
Experimental Establishment at Boscombe Down
on 5 January 1941. (Courtesy of Gladwin-Simms
Collection via www.100aircraftphotos.com)

ABOUT THE AUTHOR

Dr Alfred Price served as an aircrew officer in the Royal Air Force and,
during a flying career spanning 15 years, he logged some 4,000 flying
hours. While in the RAF he specialized and instructed in electronic
warfare and airfreighting tactics. He subsequently became a full-time
aviation historian and writer, and is acknowledged as a world authority
on the Spitfire. He has written more than 40 books on aviation
subjects, including co-authoring *Haynes Manuals* on the Supermarine
Spitfire and Avro Vulcan, and has often been asked to compile aviation
questions for the BBC television show *Mastermind*. Dr Price holds
a PhD in History, and is a fellow of the Royal Historical Society.

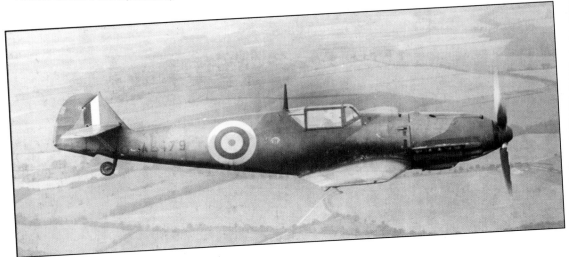